Diseases Due To Intestinal

Parasites

Dr. John H. Tilden

Kessinger Publishing's Rare Reprints

Thousands of Scarce and Hard-to-Find Books on These and other Subjects!

- Americana
- Ancient Mysteries
- Animals
- Anthropology
- Architecture
- Arts
- Astrology
- Bibliographies
- Biographies & Memoirs
- Body, Mind & Spirit
- Business & Investing
- Children & Young Adult
- Collectibles
- Comparative Religions
- Crafts & Hobbies
- Earth Sciences
- Education
- Ephemera
- Fiction
- Folklore
- Geography
- Health & Diet
- History
- Hobbies & Leisure
- Humor
- Illustrated Books
- Language & Culture
- Law
- Life Sciences
- Literature
- Medicine & Pharmacy
- Metaphysical
- Music
- Mystery & Crime
- Mythology
- Natural History
- Outdoor & Nature
- Philosophy
- Poetry
- Political Science
- Science
- Psychiatry & Psychology
- Reference
- Religion & Spiritualism
- Rhetoric
- Sacred Books
- Science Fiction
- Science & Technology
- Self-Help
- Social Sciences
- Symbolism
- Theatre & Drama
- Theology
- Travel & Explorations
- War & Military
- Women
- Yoga
- *Plus Much More!*

**We kindly invite you to view our catalog list at:
http://www.kessinger.net**

THIS ARTICLE WAS EXTRACTED FROM THE BOOK:

Impaired Health Its Cause and Cure: A Repudiation of the Conventional Treatment of Disease

BY THIS AUTHOR:

Dr. John H. Tilden

ISBN 156459954X

READ MORE ABOUT THE BOOK AT OUR WEB SITE:

http://www.kessinger.net

OR ORDER THE COMPLETE
BOOK FROM YOUR FAVORITE STORE

ISBN 156459954X

CHAPTER XI

Diseases Due To Intestinal Parasites

COMMON FORMS.—(1) Ascaris Lumbricoides; (2) Oxyuris Vermicularis; (3) Tenia Saginata; (4) Tenia Solium.

(1) Ascaris Lumbricoides.—This is a long, slender worm that inhabits the small intestines and stomach. It is one of the characteristic forms, and is frequently found in children. It looks like the common garden or angle worm, and infests children that are fed improperly. Children that are fed largely on bread, butter, syrup and sweets of all kinds, and are allowed to eat between meals until digestion is impaired or broken down, will develop these worms. It is impossible for parasites to develop in the intestines of a child or adult unless the digestive secretions are weakened to such an extent that they have no destructive influence on the ova, or eggs, of the parasites taken in with the food. It is impossible for food to be so perfectly prepared that the eggs, or ova, of parasites will not occasionally get into the alimentary canal.

(2) Oxyuris Vermicularis.—This is a small worm that infests the rectum and causes children to be very nervous. They will be continually rubbing and scratching their fundus. Such children are troubled a great deal with indigestion. Their nutrition is very poor. Their rest at night is broken. Through the day they are restless and irritable, cry easily, and are troubled with much gas and stomach derangement.

(3) Tenia Saginata.—This is the common beef tapeworm.

(4) Tenia Solium.—This is the tapeworm of pork. The same may be said of these worms as was said regarding the common worms of children. They are developed from the eggs of parasites taken in with the food, and would be digested if the digestion were perfect. It would be unreasonable to believe that those who are afflicted with tapeworm are the only people who have taken into their stomachs the ova leading to the generation of tapeworms.

Treatment.—The common treatment for worms in children is to give santonin, followed with a laxative. It is not necessary, and besides, this drug is a poison and has been known to kill. All that is necessary to get rid of these worms is to correct the diet of the child, and to give it the necessary rest by keeping it in bed until fully recovered. At first it should be kept on fruit—all the fruit it wants morning, noon, and night, but no eating between meals. This should be kept up for a week. The second week it may have toasted bread and butter, with a combination salad. As the health improves and all symptoms disappear, the fruit meal in the evening may be dropped, and toasted bread and butter, followed with milk, substituted. This should be the diet of the child until full health is established, and should be the diet of all patients suffering from intestinal parasites of any kind. Those troubled with tapeworm should fast for three days, then take the juice of a lemon in a glass of water three times a day for three days, and then live on fruit—any kind of fresh fruit—three times a day for three days. After this, have fruit for breakfast; toasted bread, butter, and fruit at noon; and a combination salad and cooked, non-starchy vegetables for the evening meal. This style of eating should be kept up until the patient can be pronounced cured—in full health.

CPSIA information can be obtained
at www.ICGtesting.com
Printed in the USA
270835LV00004B